The Pilgrims

Copyright © by Harcourt, Inc.

All rights reserved. No part of this publication may be reproduced or transmitted in any form or by any means, electronic or mechanical, including photocopy, recording, or any information storage and retrieval system, without permission in writing from the publisher.

Requests for permission to make copies of any part of the work should be addressed to School Permissions and Copyrights, Harcourt, Inc., 6277 Sea Harbor Drive, Orlando, Florida 32887-6777. Fax: 407-345-2418.

HARCOURT and the Harcourt Logo are trademarks of Harcourt, Inc., registered in the United States of America and/or other jurisdictions.

Printed in Mexico

ISBN-13: 978-0-15-351860-7
ISBN-10: 0-15-351860-X

If you have received these materials as examination copies free of charge, Harcourt School Publishers retains title to the materials and they may not be resold. Resale of examination copies is strictly prohibited and is illegal.

Possession of this publication in print format does not entitle users to convert this publication, or any portion of it, into electronic format.

3 4 5 6 7 8 9 10   050   11 10 09 08 07

Harcourt
SCHOOL PUBLISHERS

Visit *The Learning Site!* www.harcourtschool.com

Leaving Home

In the past, we lived in England.

We wanted a new place to live.

3

The <u>Mayflower</u>

Our ship was called the <u>Mayflower</u>.

The trip took many days.

New Homes

This land has all we need.
We will make new homes here.

Some day children will learn about our history.

Think and Respond

1. Why did the Pilgrims move?

2. What was the name of their ship?

3. How long did the trip take?

Activity

In a group, act out the Pilgrims coming to land. Show how they felt after their long trip.

Illustration Credits: Keiko Motoyama